A Beginner's Guide t

Campfire Tips and Techniques

Prepping and Survival Book Series

Dueep J. Singh

Mendon Cottage Books

JD-Biz Publishing

All Rights Reserved.

No part of this publication may be reproduced in any form or by any means, including scanning, photocopying, or otherwise without prior written permission from JD-Biz Corp Copyright © 2014

All Images Licensed by Fotolia and 123RF.

Disclaimer

The information is this book is provided for informational purposes only. It is not intended to be used and medical advice or a substitute for proper medical treatment by a qualified health care provider. The information is believed to be accurate as presented based on research by the author.

The contents have not been evaluated by the U.S. Food and Drug Administration or any other Government or Health Organization and the contents in this book are not to be used to treat cure or prevent disease.

The author or publisher is not responsible for the use or safety of any diet, procedure or treatment mentioned in this book. The author or publisher is not responsible for errors or omissions that may exist.

Warning

The Book is for informational purposes only and before taking on any diet, treatment or medical procedure, it is recommended to consult with your primary health care provider.

Check out some of the other Healthy Gardening Series books at Amazon.com

Gardening Series on Amazon

Check out some of the other Health Learning Series books at Amazon.com

Health Learning Series on Amazon

Table of Contents

Introduction 4
Building a Campfire 7
Picking the Right Spot 9
Building a Fire Pit 11
How much Fuel Do You Need 14
Keeping Your Fire Going in the Rain 16
What to Do with Limited Fuel? 17
Lighting the Fire Safely 18
Fire Safety 21
Putting out Your Campfire 22
Cooking Meat in a Campfire 26
Spiced Salt 29
Useful URLs 30
Conclusion 30
Author Bio 32
Publisher 42

Introduction

Ancient Greek mythology says that an adventurous and enterprising young lad named Prometheus crept into Olympus and stole one of the secrets of the Gods- Fire. As punishment, Zeus condemned him to have his liver eaten by an Eagle every morning. So while Prometheus had his liver eaten (it grew again during the night) mankind benefitted by one of Nature's most powerful gifts- Fire.

Any logical 21st century thinker is going to be entertained by this way of explaining the magic and phenomenon of fire as a treasure the Gods wanted to keep to themselves. Naturally, the ancient Greeks did not look into the much older practical use to which fire was already being put by man, much before he began dreaming up myths.

Fire was the first natural power harnessed by man which separated him from other animals eons ago. He used it for warming his camp and hearth, cooking his food, protecting him from other animals and providing him with heat and light as well as psychological comfort at night or during inclement weather.

Is it surprising then, that every civilization down the ages worshipped Fire? Not only was this power necessary for survival, but it was the holy symbol around which mankind wove his culture, rituals, and future traditional basis of religious celebrations.

Even now, Holy Fires kept burning down the ages in different places of worship follow the tradition of This is a Symbol of Hope. It should never be allowed to go out.

Down the ages, man has managed to explore even more of his surroundings, thanks to the light and comfort provided to him by a fire torch. This power has been supposed to keep evil things at bay, by mankind , for millenniums. If he had not learnt how to harness fire, he would have limited himself to one known place of shelter, where he would protect himself and members of his family and tribe, till the sun rose again.

By thanks to his knowledge with which he could now build a fire outdoors, he could be more adventurous at night. With means to make a fire and items to keep the fire alive through the night, he could stay out in the woods, or in the jungle, knowing that he was safe from predators as well as low temperatures.

And so from those first early gatherings around a common large bonfire by all the members of a tribe, millenniums ago, man still makes campfires outdoors. They are built to provide him with warmth, light and the means to protect himself from wild animals with this fearsome weapon. And also he can cook his food on this veritable gift from the Gods, instead of trying to swallow it raw.

Food and warmth...

So this book is going to give you plenty of information on how you can take best advantage of a campfire, make it, campfires, safety, campfire recipes, and how building a campfire properly can make all the difference between life and death in times of disaster or emergencies.

Building a Campfire

Experience works here...

If you find yourself outdoors in inclement weather, it is necessary that you find out the best place in which to build a campfire. Not only is this going to give you warmth and light, during the evening coming on, but it is also going to be a beacon and a signal for people to come to your aid.

Just imagine that you are building a pyramid or a teepee or an igloo. Make that triangular/conical structure with the help of small twigs and sticks. Take handfuls of dry grasses and poke it between this pyramid structure of sticks and twigs. You are going to need to get the fire burning before you can put in bigger branches of larger size.

Dry branches are best. You do not want smoky fires, do you unless of course you are sending out smoke signals?

Now light your fire by setting the grasses ablaze. These are going to set the twigs and the small branches ablaze. Once the fire has taken hold, you can add larger sticks as well as branches. The pit is going to contain the fire and prevent it from extending its boundaries.

The larger pieces of wood should be poked into the fire by pointing them towards its center. Start pushing the wood gradually into the fire, as it gets consumed by the flames.

Picking the Right Spot

Did you know that a large percentage of all the forest fires occurring in forests and natural reserves today are caused by careless campers, leaving their campfires unattended? Also, there have been many cases when people built campfires near flammable substances which caught fire.

Not only did this lead to the panic stricken campers wondering what to do next, because they did not know how to control the fire, but in such cases, many of them got trapped in fires, which went out of control.

Wildlife wardens and forest rangers consider this to be an occupational hazard of their job duties – careless campers, not knowing safety rules and not knowing where to build a fire.

So it does not matter whether you are just camping outdoors, with your family, or you are trying to get through the night stranded in the jungle – you need to know how to pick the right spot, where you can build a fire safety and without hazard to yourself or your surroundings.

If you are in a camp, and there are rules prohibiting you from building a fire there, obey the rules. The people who have built the camp at that particular site have really good reasons for making those rules.

The reasonable and sensible explanation for such a rule is that building a campfire there in possibly dry weather conditions can cause an uncontrollable fire to occur. Also, that place may be full of flammable material which may catch fire.

Never make a fire right in the middle of the jungle or in the woods, in a place where you are surrounded by trees and bushes, or even grass. Grass is one of the most flammable materials available to you in the woods. Look for a clearing.

Now just imagine that you went hunting with the evening coming on. You need a place where you can rest for the night and eat what you caught throughout the day.

You are not going to get a fire pit right in the middle of the jungle. A fire pit is a place where previous campers built fires and extinguished them after they had finished with them.

You need to build a fire pit.

Building a Fire Pit

This is of course a very elaborate fire pit, but you get the idea. Stones are used to contain the fire and to bank it.

The best site has to be about 15 feet away from shrubs, trees, branches and other materials which may be potential fire hazards. Never, ever build a fire in a place where they are low branches hanging overhead.

This is one of the mistakes which is normally made by a number of people, who have found a really fine tree under which they can take shelter. Nice roomy tree with lots of branches. They cut the branches and make their temporary or semi-permanent shelter. And then they decide to light a fire right next to their shelter.

You can visualize what is going to happen next. The shelter has been made with branches or it can also be a tent. A potentially uncontrollable fire right next to your tent is not something which you would advise your best friend, would you? That is why the fire should be in a place about 10 to 15 feet away from your shelter.

The best place to build a fire is, of course going to be a place where you have gravel or dirt on the ground. This gravel is going to come in handy when you are extinguishing your fire. All you have to do is take fistfuls of gravel and dirt and dump it on the fire, burying it tomorrow morning when you break camp.

If you have water ready at hand, water down this dirt and gravel. That muddy earth is going to dry into a hard surface. That is for preventing any potential fires starting up.

Now start digging your fire pit.

Millenniums ago, people building campfires so that their tribe could have plenty of shelter and warmth made these fires right in the middle of their camp. At night the whole tribe gathered around it, ate, sang, danced, laughed, told stories and even slept next to the fire.

The next day they made the fire in the same place because that was their fire pit. This place was protected from the wind. That meant a sudden gust of wind could not take a burning branch away from the fire and set their surroundings ablaze.

It was also at least 15 feet away from the rest of the encampment. Prepare the fire pit area by clearing all the flammable objects like leaves, grass, firewood and twigs. Make sure that there are no branches around.

Do not throw them away because you are going to use them to light the fire. You can also set the other people in your group to gathering more flammable objects like branches, dried twigs and dried grass and even the bark and wood from dead trees, if you can find them.

Just visualize the fire blazing up, when you put a branch in it. How high would the sparks go? So all right, the sparks are just sparks, and are not as powerful as flames, but the flames could go as high, could not they? So at least an area of about 10 feet in diameter should be completely clear of these objects.

Also, the vertical clearance of your fire should be about 25 feet because even though the flames may not go up to that much height, a really large fire can produce that much heat to damage surrounding branches and trees.

I remember a festive occasion, when we were celebrating a very pagan festival where the harvest is celebrated by building a huge bonfire and giving thanks to all the gods – including the fire God and the Goddess of The Harvest – for a good harvest.

The whole community gathered around a huge bonfire built in the park and a merry time was had by all. For about six hours, this fire blazed with lots of logs and other wooden items piled on it. And all of us ate, drank, danced and sang like so many civilizations have been doing down the ages to celebrate the bounty of a good harvest and the blessing of Fire.

The next evening, when we went to the park, we were shocked to see that the branches and trees up to *40 feet away* from the fire had shriveled and got burned due to the intensity of the heat. So that is why a fire should always be built away from things which can potentially get damaged by the ensuing heat.

Now it is time to start digging your pit.

Remember those Westerns that you enjoyed as a kid, where the Cowboys built fires in the evenings and had their beans and coffee prior to going to sleep in their sleeping bags? Actually in real life they started preparing to build a fire much before sunset when they found the best camping site. They then made a whole, which was about 1 feet deep. This was their fire pit. That was if they intended to stay on that site for a longer period of time.

But if their camp was temporary, and they intended to move at dawn the next day they just built a small fire in a clearing. They did not have to worry much about flammable objects in the desert.

Once the pit has been dug, you need to line it with rocks. This keeps the pit from caving in.

Till then, the other people in your group must have collected lots of natural items with which you are going to feed your fire. After you have built it, you are going to need a lot of fuel to feed it throughout the night. And remember that once night comes on, you are not going to spend your time poking in the jungle looking for fuel.

How much Fuel Do You Need

I remember my father teaching us kids woodcraft in the middle of a forest after a day spent hunting, and setting us to collect fuel for a fire. Naturally, we just gathered handfuls of grasses and twigs. We did not bother much about branches because they were so heavy to drag. Also, we were so hungry and we wanted to get to our dinners!

So he gave us a practical demonstration. He just put in the twigs and the pieces of grass into the fire, and told us to time how long it took for those objects to get consumed. They got burned in less than two minutes. Then he told us, "do the maths. Just imagine that you are spending the night outside in a forest. You need to feed the fire throughout the night. You are not going to go hunting for firewood in the middle of the night just because you did not have enough of fuel, and then there are all those bad animals and even snakes all around you in the night. So your fire burns out at 10 o'clock. What are you going to do?"

We got the hint. So remember that the more firewood you heap as fuel for your fire, the more chances you are going to have of your fire surviving till tomorrow morning.

Make your fuel fire, heap away from the fire, but easily accessible to you. In fact, the Cowboys of Western lore kept branches of firewood, right next to their sleeping bags. All they had to do during the night was just throw the nearest handy branch into the fire, when and if they woke up during the night and go off to sleep again.

Keeping Your Fire Going in the Rain

It is raining. You have not found any man-made shelter. You are cold and miserable. You have found a place where you can build a small fire. Firstly, you need to protect the fire from water.

Make a log cabin or protective cabin around your fire. Take some fuel and make a sheltering roof over the fire. You can also use a piece of plastic, or a rain jacket over the fire, which will keep the rain away.

Some days ago I bought a Mylar emergency space blanket, just to see how useful it was in inclement weather. The pros of this item is that it is extremely light. If you are dry, it is going to help keep you dry. If you are wet, and wrap this around you, the moisture trapped between this blanket and your wet clothes is going to make you more miserable and more sopping wet.

So this is best as a wind breaking shelter.

Put it over-head and use branches for insulation. Now get under that shelter and light a very small fire in a small contain space under it. It is going to smoke because of the wet wood, but that is better than having no fire at all.

What to Do with Limited Fuel?

Banking can only be successful when you have a good and hot fire burning but you find yourself running out of firewood. You are going to set a number of small logs on and across the top of the fire. They should be parallel to each other.

Allow about 2 inches of airspace and ventilation between each log. Thanks to this banking between a number of logs, you are going to have plenty of fuel to maintain a smoke-free fire. That is because there is enough of oxygen circulating through the banked grid, and the combustion is going to slow down, but the fire is going to keep burning.

You can also bank the fire by breaking any potential wind source which can make the fire flare up.

If you have built the fire in a fire pit, you may not need to bank it, because the stones lining the pit are already serving as wind-breakers. Or you can build the fire next to a dirt wall or to a rock, the surface of which is going to protect the fire from the wind.

Lighting the Fire Safely

Our ancestors did not bother much about relighting a fire because there was one fire burning somewhere throughout the day or throughout the night. They also used Flint stone to ignite sparks.

Boy Scouts can use magnifying glasses to focus the rays of the sun on a piece of paper, and keep a piece of twig handy. The moment the paper caught fire, they would have a natural twig torch. But we are talking about bad weather, cold, no sun, continuous rain, and low morale. How do we light a fire under such circumstances?

Waterproof matches are excellent things to keep in your bag. I normally keep a flint lighter – Zippo – and a Chinese manufactured cheap but top quality plastic lighter, which gives me a steady flame, even in bad weather.

I also keep candles handy. If you need a steady flame going, light a candle. Once you know that you have easy access to a flame, you will be encouraged to make your fire fast and get it going.

To prevent the candles from over-melting and the wax from overflowing, I normally treat the candles to a treatment of cold water and salt for 10 minutes before I pack them away in my camp kit. Candles and matches in a waterproofed tin are the first items you need to put in your kit, prior to going out anywhere outdoors in the woods. I slip them in my pocket along with my lightweight multipurpose Swiss Army knife and my lighter.

Never use flammable liquids like petrol, gasoline, or even diesel to keep your fire burning. These are dangerous. Lighter fluid also comes in this category.

This is another mistake which a number of people do, especially those who want to set their fires burning, like Right Now. The ensuing conflagration is going to be much more of a headache to control than the time and the effort taken to get a fire burning in a proper manner.

Also, if you are using a matchstick and the fire has taken hold, do not just throw it away after blowing it out once. Either put the matchstick into the fire and allow it to get consumed or drown it in water. Even a small spark left on the match head which got thrown away in the surrounding bushes can cause a bushfire.

In fact, one of the most serious bushfires in Australia was not caused due to natural causes, like a lightning strike on dry wood. It was caused by a trekker lighting a cigarette and then throwing the match away after blowing it out once. It took three days for that ensuing fire to be put out.

There are other fire starters in the market, which are considered to be safe ways to start fires. Cedar, Pine, and other woods have resins which are excellent softwoods, which can be placed in the fire to start it as a fuel.

I found this URL rather interesting, especially the tips written by experienced campers. And like they said, utilize some common sense and do not expect it to light a wet log, you need to have dry wood!

http://www.amazon.com/Ultimate-Survival-1WG0415BX-Blastmatch-Starter-black/dp/B0000AQLKM

Fire Safety

Prevention is better than cure anytime of the day and that is why you need to have some preventive measures ready at hand in case your fire decides to get out of control.

If you have water around in a bucket or in a container, keep it next to your fire. You can also keep the gravel and the mud which you dug up when building the fire pit at hand. Spread it around the fire pit. This is loose soil which you can kick in.

If you see vegetation, lighting up because of sparks cut off the oxygen supply by the throwing gravel or water or mud over those sparks. You may also want to be that ignited grass or vegetation with wet branches. Take care that the branches do not ignite!

A fire should never be kept unattended. In olden times, all the women and children slept right next to the fire with the Warriors, making the outer security circle. But there was always one warrior who sat next to the fire and it was his job to keep the fire burning throughout the night and keeping watch at the same time.

He never looked straight into the fire, while keeping watch. That was because this light would destroy his night vision. His job was to glance at the fire to see how much firewood was required, glance at the tribal members to see that they were sleeping comfortably and properly and then glance at his surroundings to see that no two legged or four legged foe had managed to creep up near to the camp in order to create mischief and mayhem.

Putting out Your Campfire

The campfire's work is nearly done. It is soon going to be time to extinguish it.

A campfire, whether it be a small one or a roaring one is always going to be a success in matters of doing its job of providing you with light and warmth. However, it is your duty to make sure that you do not leave your camp without extinguishing the campfire completely.

You may have read trackers hunting down outlaws and telling the sheriff and his posse – "They just broke camp about 10 minutes ago. The campfire is still warm."

Now, if those outlaws had buried the campfire in a pit and stomped upon it, the trackers could have tracked them to that particular camping site, but they would not have said that "Them varmints went off towards them thar hills, 15 minutes ago. The ashes are still warm."

There are two circumstances under which you would want to extinguish your campfire. Either you do not want it to one throughout the night, now that the jamboree around it is over and you are ready to crawl into your tent, for 40 winks or you are breaking camp.

Whatever the reason, extinguishing a campfire has to be done as carefully and all the precautions taken as when you build it in the first place.

You have to make sure that all the wood has turned into ash. That means any possible embers have no chance of lighting up at night with stray gusts of wind.

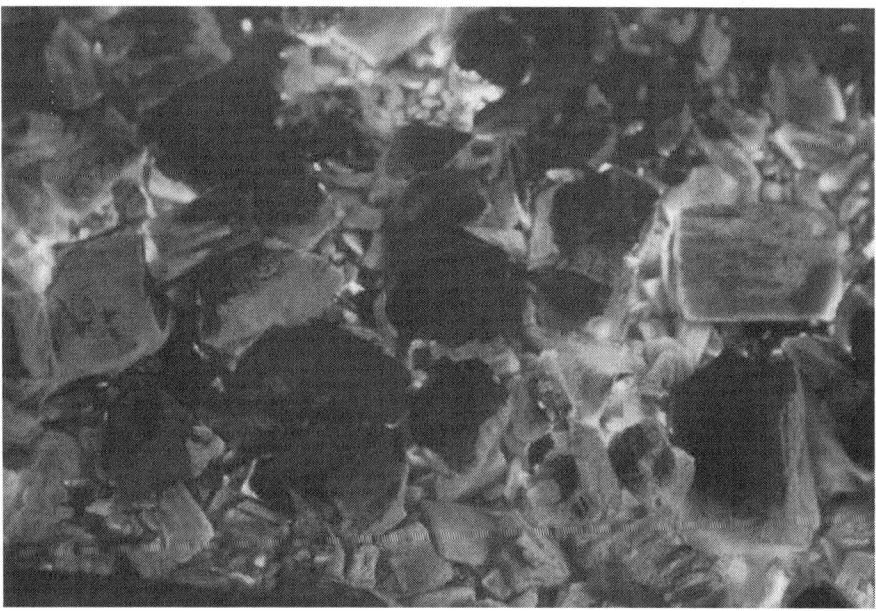

Proper dousing of the fire is done by water. Douse and completely waterlog the fire with available water. Naturally, the extinguishing flames/ashes/embers are going to hiss. Keep pouring water until there is no vestige of any fire or ember in your campfire. You are going to have an ashy and watery mess after the hissing stops.

If you have a shovel handy, just rake up all the embers and the water ashes. Turn them upside down to see if any ember managed to survive intact. Extinguish it with the shovel.

If there are any logs and branches which have not burned out completely, rake them out and make sure that there are no leftover embers. You may want to douse the logs with water if you have plenty of Fuel and nobody wants it to make another campfire.

But what if you do not have water around? Use dirt, sand, gravel, snow, or any other noninflammable object which is going to prevent the oxygen supply to the fire. Consider fire to be a somewhat human entity. No air means no life.

Make sure the fire is completely extinguished before you bury it. If that is not so, the fire is going to continue underground, especially if they are roots around. Those roots are going to reach the surface, sometime or the other and you are going to have a wildfire on your hands.

Cooking On A Fire

http://www.wikiart.org/en/norman-rockwell/hobo-and-dog-1924

Norman Rockwell's lovable hobo [let us not forget the mutt] is cooking his sausages on a fire contained in a can.[1] Of course, a can is a good utensil which you can keep along with you, to drink water. I never tried burning a fire in a can, because I never had need to. But fires for cooking can be built in containers and utensils as long as you know that the metal is going to get hot.

Do not put anything made of glass in a fire. I remember an instance when somebody wanted to do some campfire cooking outdoors and used a glass container, which happened to be present in his car. So he put a can of soup into the glass container and set it on the fire. After all the container was marketed as fireproof, he argued.

---

[1] Seriously speaking, I do not hold any chances of his twig skewer surviving a strong flame. The sausages are going to be raw, while the twig burns away. Metal skewers are best.

Well, the glass container did not melt away, but it cracked and shattered. That was because he had put it on direct heat right in the middle of a riproaring fire. So he had to throw the soup away because it was mixed with shards of glass.

Do not use aluminum cans, if you can help it. They may not burn but turn into toxic aluminum dust which is not good for your lungs.

Cooking Meat in a Campfire

The tradition of cooking meat in a campfire normally means either you cook it over an open flame like a barbecue or you cook on wood charcoal.

The traditional spit or skewer, which is normally used for cooking these pieces of meat is a flat blade sword shaped piece of steel. In olden days it was usual for warriors to just slice off a piece of meat from the hunt, skewer it on their swords and place it in the fire. They then allowed the meat to be cooked to the texture desired and ate it off the hot metal sword.

This cooking procedure is very quick, particularly when you are using a barbecue. Just take a chunk of boneless meat and cut it into bite-size pieces. Now Grease the skewer's blade lightly and carefully push it through the center of the meat chunks.

You can either place it in the charcoal and allow it to cook or you can place it over the fire, turning it occasionally, until it is done.

If you want to barbecue this meat, you may like to add some flavorings beforehand. Try out this Oriental marinade – **one large onion, minced, 4 tablespoons water, 2 ounces melted butter, three – 4 tablespoons fresh lemon**

juice, 2 ½ ounces yogurt, 1 tablespoon cumin, 1 tablespoon spiced salt [recipe given below,] 2 red chilies, depending on how hot you want the barbecue salt to taste.

Just dip the pieces of meat into all these items which have been chopped finely and mix well. If you have the time, you can keep this marinated meat in the fridge for 48 hours before barbecuing.

Grill first side brushing with the butter, once the meat has had 30 seconds or less under fierce heat. When the first side has had a total of about one minute's cooking turn and repeat on the other side. Serve hot off the coals.

Keep using the barbecue sauce over the pieces of meat, when you are grilling. My father once put a flat piece of metal over the embers of a backyard campfire, poured this marinade on that metal and placed the pieces of meat on it. He then used the skewer to turn the grilling pieces of meat. It turned out to be a really memorable meal.

What are the cooking spices I keep in my bag when cooking outdoors?

I have a McCormick mixed spices grinder with an assortment of spices in it –

http://www.mccormick.com/Spices-and-Flavors/Herbs-and-Spices

So alright, many people say that once you have used up all the spices you cannot use this grinder again. That is so not true. You can reuse this grinder again and again by just warming the Plastic cap in hot water for 10 minutes and then pulling it off. Fill the bottle with your preferred spices and then replace the lid. There you are, you have an instant grinder.

I then use my own assortment of herbs to make spiced salt.

Spiced Salt

For this you need **2 pounds of rock salt or table salt, 1 ounce of dried garlic, 2 ounces of cumin seeds, 2 ounces of coriander seeds, 2 ounces of gray or black salt, 2 ½ teaspoons full of mace and 1 ounce of black pepper.**

As peppercorns are difficult to grind in a pepper grinder, I normally crush them beforehand. But before that, I make sure that this salt is really aromatic by heating the seasonings gently in a heavy frying pan which is quite free of grease.

Place it over a low heat and stir gently. Do not allow the spices to darken in color.

The heating enhances the flavor and the aroma of the essential oils and are going to give the aromatics a much better shelf life.

Useful URLs

You may want to look at some more campfire cooking recipes, on these URLs.

http://www.tasteofhome.com/simple---delicious-magazine/easy-campfire-cooking

http://www.bbcgoodfood.com/recipes/collection/camping

You can get some more information about campfire cooking equipment on this URL.

http://www.firepit-and-grilling-guru.com/campfire-cooking-equipment.html

Conclusion

This book is a beginner's guide and introduction to the joys of building a campfire outdoors. So for all those people who did not get an opportunity to Boy Scout in their youth, here is a new opportunity for adventure – building a campfire, outdoors and cooking on it.

Live Long and Prosper!

Author Bio

Dueep Jyot Singh is a Management and IT Professional who managed to gather Postgraduate qualifications in Management and English and Degrees in Science, French and Education while pursuing different enjoyable career options like being an hospital administrator, IT,SEO and HRD Database Manager/ trainer, movie , radio and TV scriptwriter, theatre artiste and public speaker, lecturer in French, Marketing and Advertising, ex-Editor of Hearts On Fire (now known as Solstice) Books Missouri USA, advice columnist and cartoonist, publisher and Aviation School trainer, ex- moderator on Medico.in, banker, student councilor ,travelogue writer ... among other things!

One fine morning, she decided that she had enough of killing herself by Degrees and went back to her first love -- writing. It's more enjoyable! She already has 48 published academic and 14 fiction- in- different- genre books under her belt.

When she is not designing websites or making Graphic design illustrations for clients , she is browsing through old bookshops hunting for treasures, of which she has an enviable collection – including R.L. Stevenson, O.Henry, Dornford Yates, Maurice Walsh, De Maupassant, Victor Hugo, Sapper, C.N. Williamson, "Bartimeus" and the crown of her collection- Dickens "The Old Curiosity Shop," and so on... Just call her "Renaissance Woman") - collecting herbal remedies, acting like Universal Helping Hand/Agony Aunt, or escaping to her dear mountains for a bit of exploring, collecting herbs and plants and trekking.

Our books are available at

1. Amazon.com
2. Barnes and Noble
3. Itunes
4. Kobo
5. Smashwords
6. Google Play Books

Check out some of the other JD-Biz Publishing books

Gardening Series on Amazon

Health Learning Series

Country Life Books

Health Learning Series

Amazing Animal Book Series

Learn To Draw Series

How to Build and Plan Books

Entrepreneur Book Series

Publisher

JD-Biz Corp

P O Box 374

Mendon, Utah 84325

http://www.jd-biz.com/

Printed in Great Britain
by Amazon.co.uk, Ltd.,
Marston Gate.